Everyday English: Real Conversations for Real Life

By Yash d.

Table of Contents

Introduction

Purpose of the Book

Learning a language is more than just understanding grammar and vocabulary; it's about being able to communicate in real-life situations. The purpose of this book is to help you practice real-life English conversations that you might encounter every day. Whether you're traveling, working, socializing, or just running errands, this book will guide you through practical dialogues, helping you build confidence in speaking English.

By focusing on daily scenarios, this book aims to:

- Provide practical conversations you can apply immediately.

- Improve your listening and speaking skills through relatable dialogues.

- Introduce common expressions, phrases, and cultural nuances.

- Help you become more comfortable with everyday English conversations.

The more you practice these examples, the easier it will be for you to understand and respond naturally in English.

How to Use the Book

THIS BOOK IS DESIGNED to be user-friendly and practical, especially for learners at the beginner and intermediate levels. Here's how you can get the most out of it:

1. Read the Conversations: Each chapter contains sample conversations based on real-life situations. Read through these conversations carefully, paying attention to how questions are asked and answered.

2. Study the Key Phrases: After each conversation, you will find a list of key phrases and expressions. These phrases are commonly used in daily conversations, and learning them will make your communication smoother.

3. Practice Speaking: The goal is to improve your speaking skills, so try to repeat the conversations aloud. If possible, practice with a friend, a language partner, or even by yourself to get used to saying the phrases naturally.

4. Cultural Tips: Some conversations come with notes that highlight cultural norms or politeness strategies. Understanding these nuances will make you more confident and help you avoid misunderstandings in various social situations.

5. Build Confidence Gradually: Each chapter covers a different aspect of daily life. You can start with the situations that are most relevant to you and gradually expand your knowledge to other contexts. The key is consistency – the more you practice, the more comfortable you'll become.

Overview of Real-Life Conversations

REAL-LIFE CONVERSATIONS are different from textbook dialogues. They are often more spontaneous, involve informal language, and can change direction unexpectedly. This book focuses on natural interactions that occur in everyday situations, including:

- Casual Conversations: These are the simple, everyday talks we have with friends, family, and strangers. It could be a quick chat at a coffee shop, small talk with a neighbor, or catching up with a colleague.

- Transactional Conversations: These involve completing a specific task, such as ordering food, booking a ticket, or asking for directions. The goal here is to get something done, so these conversations are usually direct but polite.

- Problem-Solving Conversations: In these, you'll learn how to handle challenges like making a complaint, dealing with an issue at work, or solving an emergency situation.

- Socializing Conversations: Whether you're making new friends, attending a party, or going out for a meal, these conversations help you connect with others. Learning how to start and maintain engaging conversations in social settings is key to building relationships.

In this book, you'll explore conversations from all these categories, designed to mirror real-life situations. This will help you speak naturally, understand common phrases, and interact with confidence in both casual and formal environments.

Daily Routines

Waking Up and Morning Routines

Conversation 1: Alarm and Waking Up

- John: "Hey, Sarah, did you hear the alarm? It's already 7."

- Sarah: "Yeah, I heard it. Five more minutes, please. I'm so tired."

- John: "You said that yesterday too! We're going to be late again."

- Sarah: "Alright, alright. I'm getting up. Can you make the coffee?"

- John: "Sure, but only if you promise to actually get out of bed this time."

- Sarah: "Deal."

Conversation 2: Getting Ready for Work

- Jane: "Did you iron my shirt for today?"

- David: "I think it's still in the laundry basket."

- Jane: "What? I need it for my meeting!"

- David: "I'll iron it for you now. Do you have time to grab breakfast, or are you running late?"

- Jane: "I'll grab something on the way. Thanks for ironing it, though!"

Conversation 3: Morning Hygiene

- Emma: "You've been in the bathroom for ages! I need to brush my teeth."

- Lucas: "Just give me two more minutes. I'm almost done."

- Emma: "You said that ten minutes ago!"

- Lucas: "Alright, alright. I'm out. It's all yours."

Conversations About Breakfast

Conversation 1: Deciding What to Eat

- Max: "What do you feel like for breakfast today?"

- Lily: "I think I'll just have some cereal. I'm not that hungry."

- Max: "Really? I was thinking of making pancakes."

- Lily: "Ooh, pancakes sound good. Maybe I'll have some after all!"

- Max: "Great! I'll get the ingredients. Do you want syrup or fruit on top?"

- Lily: "Definitely syrup. Maybe some strawberries too."

Conversation 2: Making Breakfast Together

- Tom: "Can you pass me the eggs?"

- Sophie: "Here you go. How many are you using?"

- Tom: "Just two. I'm making scrambled eggs. Do you want any?"

- Sophie: "Sure, but I'll make toast. What about coffee?"

- Tom: "Already brewing. Should be ready in a few minutes."

- Sophie: "Perfect. I'll get the plates ready."

CONVERSATION 3: EATING Breakfast with Family

- Dad: "Who finished the last of the milk?"

- Anna: "It wasn't me! Maybe it was Alex."

- Alex: "What? No way, I haven't even had breakfast yet!"

- Mom: "Alright, I'll pick up more after work today. For now, we have juice."

- Anna: "Juice is fine. Can we have waffles tomorrow, though?"

- Dad: "We'll see. But let's focus on today's breakfast first."

TALKING ABOUT THE WEATHER

Conversation 1: Checking the Weather Before Leaving

- Sam: "It looks like it's going to rain today."

- Tina: "Really? I didn't check the forecast. Should I grab an umbrella?"

- Sam: "Yeah, it says there's an 80% chance of rain in the afternoon."

- Tina: "Great. I just washed my car yesterday!"

- Sam: "I know, right? Always happens. At least it's not too cold."

- Tina: "True. I'll just wear my raincoat and hope for the best."

CONVERSATION 2: WEATHER Small Talk with a Neighbor

- Neighbor: "Lovely day, isn't it?"

- Dan: "Yeah, finally some sunshine after all that rain!"

- Neighbor: "I know. I was starting to think summer was over already."

- Dan: "Let's hope this nice weather lasts a bit longer."

- Neighbor: "Fingers crossed. I've got plans for a BBQ this weekend."

- Dan: "Sounds great! Enjoy the weather while it lasts!"

CONVERSATION 3: TALKING About Unpredictable Weather

- Lisa: "Can you believe it? It was sunny five minutes ago, and now it's pouring!"

- Nick: "Yeah, I just saw that! This weather is crazy."

- Lisa: "I guess that's typical for spring. You never know what you'll get."

- Nick: "No kidding. I should start carrying an umbrella every day."

- Lisa: "Good idea. Better safe than sorry."

CASUAL GREETINGS AND Small Talk

Conversation 1: Meeting Someone in the Elevator

- Mark: "Morning! How's it going?"

- Olivia: "Hey, Mark! I'm doing well, thanks. And you?"

- Mark: "Not too bad. Just heading to a meeting."

- Olivia: "Same here. Got a busy day ahead?"

- Mark: "Yeah, tons of work. But the weekend's almost here, right?"

- Olivia: "Exactly! Just a couple more days to go."

- Mark: "Alright, see you around!"

- Olivia: "See you!"

CONVERSATION 2: GREETING a Colleague in the Office

- Emily: "Good morning, Mike! How was your weekend?"

- Mike: "Morning, Emily! It was great. I went hiking. How about you?"

- Emily: "Nice! I just relaxed and caught up on some sleep."

- Mike: "That sounds amazing. Sometimes you just need a lazy weekend."

- Emily: "Exactly. Are you ready for this week?"
- Mike: "As ready as I'll ever be!"

CONVERSATION 3: MEETING a Friend at a Café

- Rachel: "Hey! Long time no see. How have you been?"
- Adam: "Rachel! I've been good, thanks. How about you?"
- Rachel: "Doing well, just super busy with work."
- Adam: "Same here. Work has been crazy lately."
- Rachel: "I bet. Anyway, it's great to catch up. What have you been up to?"
- Adam: "Not much, just trying to survive the workweek. You?"
- Rachel: "Pretty much the same! But let's not talk about work. What are you drinking?"

CONVERSATION 4: CASUAL Chat in a Waiting Room

- Grace: "Is this your first time here?"
- Eric: "Yeah, I'm just waiting for a check-up."
- Grace: "Same here. I hope it's not a long wait."
- Eric: "Me too. I've got a meeting later, so I'm hoping to get in and out quickly."
- Grace: "Fingers crossed. So, do you come to this clinic often?"
- Eric: "Not really. Just moved to the area last month, so I'm still figuring everything out."
- Grace: "Oh, nice. Welcome! I've been here for a couple of years now."

CONVERSATION 5: BUMPING Into an Acquaintance on the Street

- Jake: "Hey, aren't you Emma's friend?"
- Liam: "Yeah, that's me! And you're Jake, right?"
- Jake: "Yep, good memory. How's it going?"
- Liam: "Pretty good! Just running some errands. You?"
- Jake: "Same here. Just grabbing a coffee. It's been a while!"
- Liam: "I know! We should all catch up sometime."
- Jake: "Definitely. I'll let Emma know."

Shopping

Conversations at the Supermarket

Scenario 1: Looking for a specific product

Customer: Excuse me, can you help me?

Staff: Sure, what are you looking for?

Customer: I'm trying to find the almond milk.

Staff: It's in aisle 4, near the cereal section.

Customer: Thank you! I've been looking everywhere.

Staff: No problem. Let me know if you need anything else.

SCENARIO 2: CHECKING out

Cashier: Hi, did you find everything you were looking for?

Customer: Yes, thanks.

Cashier: Do you have any coupons today?

Customer: No, not today.

Cashier: Your total is $45.67. Will that be cash or card?

Customer: Card, please.

Cashier: Okay, you can insert your card now.

Customer: Thanks.

Cashier: Would you like a receipt?

Customer: Yes, please.

Cashier: Here you go. Have a great day!

Customer: Thanks, you too!

ASKING FOR HELP IN a Store

Scenario 1: Finding a product

Customer: Excuse me, can you tell me where the pasta is?

Staff: Sure, it's in aisle 6, on the left side.

Customer: Great, thank you. Do you also have gluten-free pasta?

Staff: Yes, we do. It's in the same aisle, but on the bottom shelf.

Customer: Perfect, thanks for your help!

SCENARIO 2: SIZE OR color availability

Customer: Hi, do you have this sweater in a medium?

Staff: Let me check for you.

Customer: Thanks.

Staff: Sorry, it looks like we're out of medium in that color.

Customer: Do you have it in another color?

Staff: Yes, we have it in blue and green.

Customer: I'll take the blue one then.

Staff: Great choice! I'll grab it for you.

HANDLING MONEY AND Prices

Scenario 1: Asking about the price

Customer: Excuse me, how much is this shirt?

Staff: That one is $25.

Customer: Oh, I thought it was on sale.

Staff: The sale price applies only to certain colors.

Customer: I see. Is the blue one on sale?

Staff: Yes, the blue is 20% off.

Customer: Great! I'll take the blue one.

***

SCENARIO 2: CHECKING out at a cash register

Cashier: Your total is $52.89.

Customer: Does that include the sale on the shoes?

Cashier: Yes, the shoes were 30% off, and that's reflected in the total.

Customer: Okay, thanks.

Cashier: Will you be paying with cash or card?

Customer: Card, please.

Cashier: Please insert your card when you're ready.

Customer: Here you go.

Cashier: Great, your payment went through. Here's your receipt.

Customer: Thanks!

***

NEGOTIATING IN MARKETS

Scenario 1: Negotiating a price for vegetables

Customer: How much for a kilo of tomatoes?

Vendor: $3 per kilo.

Customer: That seems a bit high. Can you do $2.50?

Vendor: Hmm, how about $2.75?

Customer: Alright, I'll take two kilos at $2.75.

Vendor: Deal! Anything else you need?

Customer: No, that's it. Thank you!

***

SCENARIO 2: BUYING handmade goods

Customer: I love this scarf. How much is it?

Vendor: It's $40.

Customer: That's a bit expensive for me. Can you do $30?

Vendor: I can go down to $35, but that's the lowest I can offer.

Customer: Okay, $35 works for me.

Vendor: Great, you've made a good choice!

———◦———

SCENARIO 3: ASKING for a discount on multiple items

Customer: If I buy two of these, can you give me a discount?

Vendor: Well, they're normally $20 each, but I can give you both for $35.

Customer: Could you do $30 for both?

Vendor: $32, and you have a deal.

Customer: Okay, $32 it is! Thanks for working with me.

Vendor: No problem, enjoy your new items!

Traveling

Booking Tickets (Plane, Train, Bus)

At the Airline Counter

Customer: Hi, I'd like to book a ticket to New York, please.

Agent: Sure! When do you want to travel?

Customer: I'm looking to fly next Friday.

Agent: We have flights at 10 AM and 3 PM. Which one do you prefer?

Customer: I'll take the 10 AM flight.

Agent: Great! I'll need your ID and payment method.

Customer: Here's my ID and credit card.

Agent: Thank you! You're all set. Enjoy your trip!

At the Train Station

Customer: Hello, can I get a ticket to Chicago?

Ticket Agent: Of course! When do you want to leave?

Customer: I'd like to leave tomorrow morning.

Ticket Agent: We have a train at 8 AM. Does that work for you?

Customer: Yes, that's perfect. How much is it?

Ticket Agent: That will be $50.

Customer: Here you go.

Ticket Agent: Thank you! Here's your ticket.

AT THE BUS STATION

Customer: Hi! I need a ticket to San Francisco.

Bus Driver: When do you want to leave?

Customer: Tomorrow evening, if possible.

Bus Driver: We have a bus at 6 PM. Do you want a one-way ticket?

Customer: Yes, please.

Bus Driver: That'll be $35.

Customer: Here's my cash.

Bus Driver: Thank you! Enjoy your ride!

Asking for Directions

On the Street

Tourist: Excuse me, can you help me? I'm looking for the nearest subway station.

Local: Sure! Just go straight down this road and take a left at the traffic light.

Tourist: How far is it from here?

Local: It's about a five-minute walk.

Tourist: Thank you so much!

Local: You're welcome! Have a great day!

In a Mall

Shopper: Hi! Can you tell me where the restrooms are?

Employee: Of course! They're on the second floor, near the food court.

Shopper: Thank you! Is there an elevator?

Employee: Yes, right around the corner.

Shopper: Great, thanks again!

AT A TOURIST INFORMATION Center

Tourist: Hi! Could you point me to the museum?

Staff: Absolutely! It's just two blocks away, straight ahead.

Tourist: Is it within walking distance?

Staff: Yes, you can easily walk there in about ten minutes.

Tourist: Awesome, thank you!

Conversations at the Hotel

At the Reception Desk

Guest: Hello, I have a reservation under the name Smith.

Receptionist: Welcome, Mr. Smith! Let me check that for you.

Guest: Thank you.

Receptionist: Yes, I found it. You're in room 305. Here's your key card.

Guest: What time is checkout?

Receptionist: Checkout is at 11 AM. Enjoy your stay!

In the Hotel Lobby

Guest: Hi, could you help me with my luggage?

Bellhop: Of course! Where are you headed?

Guest: To room 305.

Bellhop: Right this way.

Guest: Thank you! Can I get extra towels sent to my room?

Bellhop: Absolutely! I'll have them delivered shortly.

At the Concierge Desk

Guest: Hi, can you recommend a good restaurant nearby?

Concierge: Sure! There's a great Italian place just a block away.

Guest: What's it called?

Concierge: It's called Bella Italia.

Guest: Sounds good! Do I need a reservation?

Concierge: It's a busy spot, so I'd recommend it. Would you like me to book a table for you?

Guest: Yes, please!

ORDERING FOOD AT A Restaurant

At a Restaurant Table

Server: Hi there! Can I get you started with something to drink?

Customer: Yes, I'd like a glass of water, please.

Server: Sure! Are you ready to order?

Customer: Yes, I'll have the chicken pasta.

Server: Excellent choice! Would you like anything else?

Customer: Just a side salad, please.

Server: Got it! I'll be right back with your drinks.

AT A CAFÉ

Customer: Hi! I'd like to order a cappuccino.

Barista: What size would you like?

Customer: A medium, please.

Barista: Would you like anything to eat with that?

Customer: Yes, I'll have a blueberry muffin.

Barista: Great! That'll be $7.50.

AT A FAST-FOOD RESTAURANT

Customer: Hello! I'd like a cheeseburger combo.

Cashier: Would you like fries or a salad with that?

Customer: Fries, please. And a Coke to drink.

Cashier: That'll be $8.50. Drive-thru or dine-in?

Customer: Dine-in.

Cashier: Thank you! Your order will be ready shortly.

At Work

Office Introductions

Emily: Hi, I'm Emily. I just started as the new marketing coordinator.

James: Nice to meet you, Emily! I'm James, the graphic designer. How are you finding it so far?

Emily: It's great! Everyone has been really welcoming.

James: That's good to hear. If you need any help settling in, just let me know!

Emily: Thanks, I appreciate that!

Participating in Meetings

Sarah: Good morning, everyone. Let's get started with today's agenda. First, we'll discuss the new project timelines.

Michael: I think it would be helpful to review the last project's timeline to see what adjustments we need to make.

Sarah: Great idea, Michael. Let's take a look at that. How did the last project go in terms of deadlines?

Lisa: We missed a few deadlines because of unforeseen issues. We should account for that in our planning.

Michael: Agreed. I propose we add some buffer time to each phase.

Sarah: Sounds reasonable. Let's document that suggestion.

Asking for Assistance

Tom: Hi, Clara. Do you have a moment?

Clara: Sure, Tom! What do you need help with?

Tom: I'm having trouble with the sales report. Could you explain how to pull the data from the new software?

Clara: Of course! Let me show you. First, you need to log in and go to the reports section.

Tom: Okay, I see it. What's next?

Clara: Click on "Sales Overview" and then select the date range you need.

Tom: Got it! Thanks so much for your help.

Clara: No problem! Let me know if you need anything else.

EMAIL COMMUNICATION

Subject: Request for Project Update

From: Emily <emily@example.com>

To: Team <team@example.com>

Hi Team,

I hope this message finds you well. I wanted to check in on the status of the current marketing campaign. Could everyone please provide a quick update by the end of the day?

Thanks!

Best,

Emily

Subject: Re: Request for Project Update

From: James <james@example.com>

To: Emily <emily@example.com>

Hi Emily,

I'm on track with the graphics and expect to have everything ready by Wednesday. Let me know if there's anything specific you'd like to see!

Best,

James

⟿ ◈ ⟾

PHONE COMMUNICATION

Emily: (on the phone) Hi, this is Emily from marketing. Can I speak to Mr. Thompson, please?

Receptionist: Sure, may I ask what this is regarding?

Emily: I'd like to discuss the upcoming advertisement campaign.

Receptionist: One moment, please. I'll transfer you.

Mr. Thompson: Hello, this is Mr. Thompson.

Emily: Hi, Mr. Thompson! This is Emily from marketing. I wanted to go over some ideas for the campaign.

Mr. Thompson: Great! I'm looking forward to hearing them.

Emily: Perfect! I think we should focus on social media strategies.

Socializing

Meeting New People

Emma: Hi, I'm Emma! What's your name?

Liam: Nice to meet you, Emma. I'm Liam.

Emma: So, what do you do for a living?

Liam: I work in graphic design. How about you?

Emma: I'm a teacher. I teach elementary school.

Liam: That's great! What subject do you enjoy teaching the most?

Emma: I love teaching art. It's so much fun to see the kids express themselves.

Liam: I can imagine! Do you have any upcoming projects?

Emma: Yes, we're working on a mural for the school. It should be exciting!

Liam: Sounds awesome! I'd love to see it when it's done.

INVITING FRIENDS FOR Coffee/Dinner

Ava: Hey, Ben! Are you free this weekend?

Ben: Hi, Ava! I think I am. What's up?

Ava: I was thinking of grabbing coffee on Saturday. Want to join?

Ben: That sounds great! What time were you thinking?

Ava: How about 2 PM at that new café downtown?

Ben: Perfect! I've been wanting to try it out.

Ava: Awesome! Let's meet there then.

Ben: Can't wait! See you Saturday.

SOPHIA: HEY, MIA! WOULD you like to come over for dinner this Friday?

Mia: I'd love that! What time should I come?

Sophia: How about 7 PM?

Mia: Sounds good! What are you cooking?

Sophia: I'm planning to make pasta.

Mia: Yum! I'm looking forward to it.

Sophia: Great! I'll have some dessert ready too.

Mia: You know me too well!

TALKING ABOUT HOBBIES and Interests

Jake: So, what do you like to do in your free time?

Lily: I really enjoy painting. How about you?

Jake: I'm into hiking. I love exploring nature.

Lily: That sounds amazing! Do you have a favorite hiking spot?

Jake: Yes, there's a beautiful trail about an hour from here.

Lily: I'd love to check it out sometime!

Jake: You should come with me next time!

Lily: I'd be up for that.

OLIVER: WHAT HOBBIES do you have, Sarah?

Sarah: I love reading and writing in my journal.

Oliver: That's cool! What's your favorite genre?

Sarah: I really enjoy fantasy. How about you?

Oliver: I'm into photography. I love capturing landscapes.

Sarah: That sounds fascinating! Do you have a favorite photo you've taken?

Oliver: Yes, one from my last trip to the mountains. I'd love to show you!

Sarah: I'd love to see it!

———◉———

CELEBRATIONS (BIRTHDAYS, Holidays)

Emily: Are you doing anything special for your birthday this year?

Noah: Yes, I'm planning a small party at my place. Want to come?

Emily: I'd love to! What should I bring?

Noah: Just bring yourself and maybe some snacks if you'd like.

Emily: Sounds good! What time should I arrive?

Noah: Let's say 6 PM.

Emily: Great! I can't wait to celebrate with you!

Noah: Me too! It'll be fun!

———◉———

SOPHIE: HOW DO YOU usually celebrate the holidays?

Aiden: We have a big family gathering every year. What about you?

Sophie: My family loves to cook together and watch holiday movies.

Aiden: That sounds cozy! Do you have a favorite holiday movie?

Sophie: Yes, "Home Alone" is a classic!

Aiden: I love that one too!

Sophie: Maybe we could watch it together sometime!

Aiden: Definitely! I'd enjoy that.

CHLOE: ARE YOU PLANNING anything for New Year's Eve?

Jack: Yeah, I'm having a few friends over for a countdown party.

Chloe: That sounds fun! Can I join?

Jack: Of course! The more, the merrier!

Chloe: Should I bring anything?

Jack: Just bring your favorite drink!

Chloe: Will do! I can't wait!

Jack: Same here!

Health and Emergencies

Going to the Doctor

Patient: Hi, I have an appointment at 2 PM.

Receptionist: Welcome! Can I have your name, please?

Patient: Sure, it's Alex Johnson.

Receptionist: Thank you, Alex. Please fill out this form while you wait.

Patient: No problem. How long is the wait usually?

Receptionist: It's about 15-20 minutes.

Patient: Okay, thanks!

Doctor: Hi, Alex! I'm Dr. Smith. What brings you in today?

Patient: I've been feeling really tired and I have a sore throat.

Doctor: How long have you been feeling this way?

Patient: About a week now.

Doctor: Have you had any fever or other symptoms?

Patient: Yes, I had a slight fever yesterday and some headaches.

Doctor: Let's take a look. Please open your mouth wide.

Talking About Symptoms

Patient: I think I might have a cold.

Doctor: What symptoms are you experiencing?

Patient: I have a runny nose and a cough.

Doctor: Any fever or body aches?

Patient: No fever, but my muscles feel sore.

Doctor: Have you been drinking enough fluids?

Patient: Not really. I've been so tired.

Doctor: It's important to stay hydrated. I recommend rest and over-the-counter medication.

Handling Emergencies

Caller: 911, what's your emergency?

Caller: I need help! My friend just fainted.

Operator: Is he breathing?

Caller: Yes, but he's unresponsive.

Operator: Stay calm. Is he lying down on his back?

Caller: Yes.

Operator: Check for signs of breathing.

Caller: He's breathing slowly.

Operator: Good. Stay with him until help arrives.

PHARMACY CONVERSATIONS

Customer: Hi, I'd like to pick up a prescription for Emily Carter.

Pharmacist: Sure! Can I see your ID, please?

Customer: Here you go.

Pharmacist: Thank you! This is for an antibiotic. Make sure to take it with food.

Customer: Are there any side effects I should watch for?

Pharmacist: Common side effects include nausea and dizziness. If she experiences anything severe, call us.

Customer: Got it. How often does she need to take it?

Pharmacist: Twice a day for seven days.

Customer: Thanks for your help!

Dealing with Problems

Complaints (Service Issues, Deliveries)

Customer: Hi, I ordered a blender last week, but it hasn't arrived yet.

Support: I'm sorry to hear that. Can I have your order number, please?

Customer: Sure, it's 123456.

Support: Thank you. Let me check the status. It looks like there was a delay in shipping.

Customer: That's frustrating. I needed it for a party this weekend.

Support: I completely understand. We'll expedite the shipping and ensure it arrives by tomorrow.

Customer: Thank you! I appreciate that.

CUSTOMER: HELLO, I received the wrong item in my order.

Support: I'm sorry about that. Can you tell me what you received?

Customer: I ordered a pair of shoes, but I got a jacket instead.

Support: Thank you for letting us know. I can arrange for the jacket to be returned and send you the shoes.

Customer: That sounds good. How long will that take?

Support: You'll receive the correct item in 3-5 business days once we process the return.

Customer: Okay, thank you for your help!

———◦———

CUSTOMER SUPPORT CONVERSATIONS

Customer: Hi, I need help with my internet connection. It's been really slow.

Support: I'm sorry to hear that. Can you tell me when the issue started?

Customer: It started a couple of days ago. I can barely stream anything.

Support: Let me check your account. It looks like there's an outage in your area.

Customer: Oh no! When will it be fixed?

Support: The team is working on it, and it should be resolved by tomorrow evening.

Customer: Thanks for the update. I'll wait for it to be fixed.

Customer: I have a problem with my billing statement.

Support: I'm here to help. What seems to be the issue?

Customer: I was charged twice for my last payment.

Support: Let me pull up your account. Yes, I see the duplicate charge.

Customer: Can you fix that?

Support: Absolutely. I'll process a refund for the extra charge right away.

Customer: Thank you! I appreciate it.

———◦———

RESOLVING CONFLICTS Politely

Person A: Hey, I noticed you borrowed my book without asking.

Person B: I'm really sorry about that. I thought I could return it soon.

Person A: I understand, but it's important to me. Can we agree that you ask next time?

Person B: Of course! I'll make sure to ask first next time.

Person A: Thanks, I appreciate it.

Person A: I felt like you were interrupting me in the meeting earlier.

Person B: I didn't mean to interrupt. I just wanted to share my thoughts.

Person A: I understand, but it's important for everyone to finish their points.

Person B: You're right. I'll be more mindful of that in the future.

Person A: Thank you! I appreciate your understanding.

Person A: I think we need to discuss how we're dividing the work on this project.

Person B: I agree. I've felt overwhelmed lately.

Person A: I didn't realize. Let's reassign some tasks to make it more balanced.

Person B: That would really help. Thank you for being open to this.

Person A: Of course! We're a team.

——⬥——

PERSON A: I HEARD SOME rumors about my work performance. Can we talk about it?

Manager: I appreciate you bringing this up. Let's discuss any concerns you have.

Person A: I just want to know if there are specific areas I need to improve.

Manager: I think you're doing well, but there's always room for growth.

Person A: Thank you for your feedback. I'll work on it.

Phrases and Expressions

Common Idioms in Daily Life

1. Break the ice

Person A: "I was really nervous at the party."

Person B: "Yeah, it can be awkward. I usually try to break the ice with a joke."

2. Hit the nail on the head

Person A: "I think the main issue is communication."

Person B: "Exactly! You hit the nail on the head."

3. A piece of cake

Person A: "How was the exam?"

Person B: "It was a piece of cake! I finished in 30 minutes."

4. Let the cat out of the bag

Person A: "Did you hear about Sarah's surprise party?"

Person B: "Oh no! Who let the cat out of the bag?"

5. Spill the beans

Person A: "Are you going to tell me what happened?"

Person B: "Alright, I'll spill the beans. I got the job!"

6. Under the weather

Person A: "Why didn't you come to the meeting?"

Person B: "I was feeling a bit under the weather."

7. Cost an arm and a leg

Person A: "How much was the new phone?"

Person B: "It cost an arm and a leg, but it's worth it!"

8. Jump on the bandwagon

Person A: "Everyone is investing in stocks."

Person B: "I might jump on the bandwagon too!"

9. Call it a day

Person A: "It's getting late. Should we call it a day?"

Person B: "Yeah, I think we've done enough."

10. Burn the midnight oil

Person A: "How did you finish that project?"

Person B: "I had to burn the midnight oil to get it done."

Expressions for Politeness and Respect

1. Please

Person A: "Could you pass me the salt, please?"

Person B: "Sure, here you go!"

2. Thank you

Person A: "I really appreciate your help!"

Person B: "You're welcome! I'm glad I could assist."

3. Excuse me

Person A: "Excuse me, do you have a moment?"

Person B: "Of course! What do you need?"

4. I'm sorry

Person A: "I'm sorry for interrupting you."

Person B: "No problem at all! What's on your mind?"

5. May I...?

Person A: "May I take your order?"

Person B: "Yes, I'd like a coffee, please."

6. Would you mind...?

Person A: "Would you mind closing the window?"

Person B: "Not at all! I'll do it right now."

7. It would be great if...

Person A: "It would be great if you could join us for dinner."

Person B: "I'd love to! Thank you for the invitation."

8. I appreciate it

Person A: "Thanks for the advice."

Person B: "I appreciate it, and I'm happy to help."

9. If it's not too much trouble

Person A: "If it's not too much trouble, could you send me that file?"

Person B: "Of course, I'll send it right away!"

10. Thank you for your understanding

Person A: "I'm sorry for the delay."

Person B: "Thank you for your understanding."

CULTURAL CONSIDERATIONS

1. Personal Space

Person A: "In my culture, we stand quite close when talking."

Person B: "That's interesting! Here, we usually keep a bit of distance."

2. Greetings

Person A: "In my country, we greet everyone with a kiss."

Person B: "Wow! We usually just shake hands here."

3. Dining Etiquette

Person A: "Is it rude to start eating before everyone is served?"

Person B: "Yes, we usually wait until the host says 'dig in.'"

4. Tipping

Person A: "Do you tip at restaurants?"

Person B: "Yes, it's customary to tip around 15-20%."

5. Gift Giving

Person A: "Is it appropriate to open gifts in front of the giver?"

Person B: "It depends; in some cultures, it's expected, while in others, it's not."

6. Silence

Person A: "Why is everyone so quiet during the meeting?"

Person B: "In some cultures, silence is a sign of respect."

7. Asking Questions

Person A: "In my culture, asking questions shows interest."

Person B: "Here, it can sometimes be seen as intrusive."

8. Humor

Person A: "I love telling jokes, but I've noticed some don't get my humor."

Person B: "Humor can vary a lot between cultures!"

9. Direct vs. Indirect Communication

Person A: "I prefer being direct in conversations."

Person B: "I understand; some cultures value indirect communication."

10. Formality

Person A: "When should I use titles like 'Mr.' or 'Dr.'?"

Person B: "It's best to use them until you're invited to be more casual."

Telephonic Conversion

1. Calling for an Appointment (Doctor's Office)

Receptionist:

Hello, thank you for calling Greenfield Medical Clinic. How may I assist you?

Caller:

Hi, I'd like to schedule an appointment with Dr. Smith, please.

Receptionist:

Sure. Can I have your name, please?

Caller:

Yes, it's Jessica Thompson.

Receptionist:

Alright, Jessica. Are you a new patient or an existing one?

Caller:

I'm an existing patient. I've been seeing Dr. Smith for a couple of months.

Receptionist:

Great. When would you like to come in?

Caller:

Do you have any availability this week, maybe Thursday?

Receptionist:

Let me check. Yes, we have an opening at 10 AM on Thursday. Does that work for you?

Caller:

That sounds perfect, thank you.

Receptionist:

You're all set for Thursday at 10 AM. We'll see you then, Jessica!

Caller:

Thank you so much! See you then.

<hr>

2. ORDERING FOOD OVER the Phone (Takeaway/Restaurant)

Customer:

Hello, I'd like to place an order for delivery, please.

Restaurant Staff:

Of course! May I have your name and address?

Customer:

It's Michael, and my address is 123 Main Street, Apartment 2B.

Restaurant Staff:

Got it, Michael. What would you like to order?

Customer:

I'll take a large pepperoni pizza and an order of garlic bread.

Restaurant Staff:

Would you like anything to drink with that?

Customer:

Yes, a bottle of Coke, please.

Restaurant Staff:

Alright. That'll be one large pepperoni pizza, garlic bread, and a bottle of Coke. The total comes to $22.50, and the delivery will take about 30-40 minutes.

Customer:

Sounds good. Can I pay with a card?

Restaurant Staff:

Yes, you can pay when the delivery arrives or over the phone now.

Customer:

I'll pay when the delivery arrives. Thank you!

Restaurant Staff:

Thank you for your order, Michael. Have a great day!

***

3. CALLING CUSTOMER Service (Internet Issues)

Customer:

Hi, I'm calling because I'm having some issues with my internet connection. It's been down since this morning.

Support Agent:

I'm sorry to hear that! Can I have your account number, please?

Customer:

Sure, it's 12345678.

Support Agent:

Thank you. Let me take a look. I see there's a network outage in your area. Our technicians are working on it, and it should be resolved within the next few hours.

Customer:

Oh, okay. I just wanted to make sure it wasn't something on my end.

Support Agent:

Nope, it's on our side. We apologize for the inconvenience. Is there anything else I can help you with?

Customer:

No, that's all for now. Thanks for your help!

Support Agent:

You're welcome! Have a great day, and we appreciate your patience.

---

4. SCHEDULING A MEETING (Workplace Call)

Caller:

Hi, Sarah. It's James. Do you have a minute to talk about next week's meeting?

Sarah:

Sure, James. What's on your mind?

James:

I wanted to confirm the time. I was thinking we could meet at 2 PM on Tuesday. Does that work for you?

Sarah:

Let me check my calendar... Yes, that works for me.

James:

Great. I'll send a calendar invite, and we can go over the project updates.

Sarah:

Perfect. Anything else we need to prepare beforehand?

James:

Just make sure to have your latest reports ready, and we'll be good to go.

Sarah:

Sounds good. Thanks, James.

James:

No problem. See you on Tuesday!

5. CALLING A FRIEND to Make Plans

Caller:

Hey, Karen! It's been a while. How have you been?

Karen:

Hi, Mike! I've been great. How about you?

Caller:

I'm doing well, thanks. I was wondering if you're free this weekend. Maybe we could grab lunch or go for a hike?

Karen:

That sounds fun! I'm actually free on Saturday. Would that work for you?

Caller:

Saturday works for me too. How about we meet around 12 PM for lunch and then go for a hike afterward?

Karen:

That sounds perfect. Do you have a place in mind for lunch?

Caller:

How about that new café downtown? I've heard good things about it.

Karen:

I've been wanting to try that place! Let's do it.

Caller:

Awesome! I'll see you at 12 on Saturday then.

Karen:

Looking forward to it! See you then.

---

6. CALLING A HOTEL to Make a Reservation

Caller:

Good afternoon, I'd like to make a reservation for next weekend, please.

Hotel Staff:

Certainly. May I have your name and the dates you'd like to stay?

Caller:

Sure, it's Anna Lee, and I'd like to stay from Friday to Sunday, the 10th to the 12th.

Hotel Staff:

Let me check availability... Yes, we have a few rooms available. Would you prefer a standard room or a suite?

Caller:

A standard room will be fine.

Hotel Staff:

Alright. I have a standard room available for $150 per night. Should I go ahead and book it for you?

Caller:

Yes, please.

Hotel Staff:

Great. I'll need a credit card to hold the reservation.

Caller:

Okay, let me give you my details.

Hotel Staff:

Thank you, Ms. Lee. Your reservation is confirmed. We look forward to welcoming you next weekend.

Caller:

Thank you! See you then.

---

7. CALLING FOR A JOB Interview (Recruitment)

Recruiter:

Hello, this is Sarah from HR Solutions. Am I speaking with Mr. Patel?

Candidate:

Yes, this is Raj Patel.

Recruiter:

Great! I'm calling to follow up on your application for the Marketing Specialist position. We'd love to schedule an interview with you. Are you available next week?

Candidate:

Yes, I'm available. What day would work for you?

Recruiter:

How about Wednesday at 10 AM?

Candidate:

That works for me. Will it be an in-person interview, or is it over the phone?

Recruiter:

It will be a virtual interview via Zoom. I'll send you the meeting link shortly.

Candidate:

Perfect, thank you. I'll be ready!

Recruiter:

Great, Raj. We're looking forward to speaking with you.

---

8. ASKING FOR DIRECTIONS Over the Phone

Caller:

Hi, I'm trying to find your office, but I'm a little lost. Could you give me some directions?

Office Receptionist:

Of course! Where are you now?

Caller:

I'm near 5th Avenue, but I'm not sure which way to go.

Office Receptionist:

Okay, from 5th Avenue, walk two blocks north, and you'll see a big red building on your left. Our office is in that building on the third floor.

Caller:

Got it. Two blocks north and then the red building. Thanks so much!

Office Receptionist:

You're welcome! See you soon.

---

9. RESCHEDULING A DELIVERY

Customer:

Hi, I'm calling to reschedule a delivery. It was supposed to arrive tomorrow, but I won't be home.

Delivery Service:

No problem! Can I have your order number?

Customer:

Sure, it's 987654.

Delivery Service:

Thank you. When would you like to reschedule the delivery for?

Customer:

Can we do Friday instead?

Delivery Service:

Friday works. Would you prefer morning or afternoon delivery?

Customer:

Afternoon, please.

Delivery Service:

Alright, your delivery has been rescheduled for Friday afternoon. Is there anything else I can assist you with?

Customer:

No, that's all. Thanks for your help!

10. CALLING A TAXI SERVICE

Caller:

Hi, I need to book a taxi, please.

Taxi Service:

Sure! Where would you like to be picked up?

Caller:

I'm at 200 Elm Street.

Taxi Service:

And where are you headed?

Caller:

To the airport, Terminal 3.

Taxi Service:

Got it. A taxi will be there in about 10 minutes.

Caller:

Great, thank you!

These conversations touch on a wide range of everyday situations, from making appointments and placing orders to arranging meetings and scheduling deliveries. Practicing such dialogues will help English learners gain confidence in managing real-life conversations on the phone. Each scenario is designed to be as practical

Job Interview Conversation

Interviewer (John):

Good morning, Sarah. Thanks for coming in today.

Candidate (Sarah):

Good morning, John. Thanks for having me.

John:

So, let's start with you telling me a bit about yourself.

Sarah:

Sure! My name's Sarah, and I've been working in marketing for the past five years. I graduated with a degree in communications and started my career as a content writer. Over time, I transitioned into digital marketing, and my most recent role was as a social media manager at XYZ Company.

John:

Interesting. What made you shift from content writing to digital marketing?

Sarah:

Well, I've always been interested in the broader picture of how content fits into a marketing strategy. Writing is just one part of it. I started exploring SEO and social media, and I really enjoyed the challenge of combining creativity with data analysis. It felt like a natural progression for me to dive deeper into the digital side of things.

John:

That makes sense. Can you tell me more about your last role at XYZ Company? What were your main responsibilities?

Sarah:

Sure! At XYZ, I was responsible for developing the company's social media strategy across platforms like Instagram, Facebook, and LinkedIn. I created content calendars, managed ad campaigns, and analyzed performance metrics to optimize future content. I also collaborated with the design team to ensure everything was aligned with our brand's visual identity.

John:

Sounds like you were wearing a lot of hats. What would you say was the most challenging part of that role?

Sarah:

Definitely juggling multiple campaigns at once. Sometimes we had seasonal promotions, product launches, and routine content all happening at the same time. It was a lot to manage, but I learned how to prioritize and delegate tasks to stay on top of everything.

John:

Time management is key in a role like that. Speaking of challenges, can you describe a situation where you had to solve a major problem?

Sarah:

Yes, one situation comes to mind. We were launching a new product line, and two days before the launch, we realized there was a mistake in the promotional material – the pricing was incorrect. I immediately gathered the team, and we brainstormed solutions. We quickly edited and re-uploaded the content on all platforms, but we also created a backup plan with discount codes in case any customers saw the original price and felt confused. Fortunately, we managed to fix everything before it became a bigger issue.

John:

That's impressive. It shows quick thinking under pressure. Now, let's talk about working with a team. How do you typically approach collaboration?

Sarah:

I believe collaboration is about communication and respect. I make sure to listen to everyone's ideas, and I'm not afraid to ask questions or offer feedback. I enjoy brainstorming sessions because I think that's when some of the best ideas come out. I'm also comfortable taking the lead when needed but always make sure everyone feels involved.

John:

Teamwork is so important, especially in a fast-paced environment. How do you handle conflict within a team?

Sarah:

I try to address conflict head-on but in a calm and constructive way. I've found that most issues stem from miscommunication, so I always try to clarify everyone's perspective first. I also focus on finding a solution rather than pointing fingers. For example, during a campaign, there was a misunderstanding between me and the design team about deadlines. I brought it up in our next meeting and suggested a better workflow for the future, which everyone appreciated.

John:

That's a great approach. Now, looking at this role, what interests you the most about it?

Sarah:

I'm really excited about the opportunity to work on larger-scale campaigns. I've managed social media for mid-sized companies, but your company's global presence offers a chance to challenge myself and grow. I'm also drawn to the innovative projects your team is working on – especially around influencer marketing, which is an area I'm passionate about.

John:

It's good to hear you're enthusiastic about the direction we're heading. We're definitely focusing more on influencer marketing. What experience do you have in that area?

Sarah:

I've worked with micro-influencers in the past, helping to promote our products through sponsored content and giveaways. One of my favorite campaigns was with a lifestyle blogger who created a series of Instagram posts and stories for our fall collection. The engagement was great, and we saw a spike in sales. I'd love to expand on that and work with bigger names in the industry.

John:

It sounds like you've had some success with influencer marketing. How do you stay current with trends in digital marketing?

Sarah:

I'm always reading industry blogs, attending webinars, and taking online courses. Marketing changes so quickly, so I make it a priority to stay up-to-date. I'm particularly interested in the role of AI in digital marketing right now, and I've been exploring how automation tools can streamline content creation and analysis.

John:

That's great. We're definitely moving toward more automation here as well. Let's switch gears for a moment. What do you enjoy doing outside of work?

Sarah:

I'm really into photography and hiking. On weekends, I try to get out of the city and explore nature. It helps me clear my head and also gives me a lot of creative inspiration.

John:

That sounds like a nice balance. Now, back to the role. Where do you see yourself in the next few years?

Sarah:

I'd like to continue developing my skills in digital marketing and eventually move into a leadership position, managing a larger team. I'm also interested in expanding my knowledge in areas like data analytics and marketing strategy, so I see myself contributing more to high-level decision-making.

John:

It's always good to have a long-term vision. What would you say are your biggest strengths and weaknesses?

Sarah:

I'd say my strengths are adaptability and creativity. I can quickly adjust to changes and come up with new ideas on the fly. As for weaknesses, I sometimes struggle with delegating because I want to make sure everything is done right, but I'm working on trusting my team more and letting go of control.

John:

That's an honest answer, and it's good to be aware of areas for improvement. Lastly, do you have any questions for me?

Sarah:

Yes, I do. Could you tell me more about the team I'd be working with and what a typical day might look like in this role?

John:

Absolutely. You'd be working closely with our marketing director and a small team of content creators and designers. We usually start the day with a brief stand-up meeting to go over priorities, then the rest of the day is spent working on campaigns, reviewing performance metrics, and collaborating with different departments. We like to keep things dynamic, so no two days are exactly the same.

Sarah:

That sounds like an exciting environment to be part of. Thank you for the insight.

John:

No problem. Well, Sarah, I think we've covered everything. Thanks again for coming in today.

Sarah:

Thank you, John. I really appreciate the opportunity to speak with you.

John:

You're welcome. We'll be in touch soon regarding next steps.

Sarah:

Great, I look forward to hearing from you. Have a good day!

John:

You too, Sarah. Take care!

***

THIS CONVERSATION OFFERS a real-life scenario of how a job interview flows in everyday English, showcasing professional yet conversational language.

Dining Out and Ordering Food

1. Vocabulary for Restaurant Settings:

Host: The person who greets you and takes you to your table.

Waiter/Waitress: The person who takes your order and serves your food.

Menu: The list of food and drinks available.

Appetizer: A small dish served before the main meal.

Entrée: The main course of the meal.

Dessert: Sweet food served at the end of a meal.

Bill/Check: The amount you need to pay for the meal.

Reservation: Booking a table in advance.

2. How to Order Food and Drinks

Scenario 1: Ordering at a Casual Restaurant

Waiter: Hello! Welcome to Bella's Café. Are you ready to order, or would you like a few minutes?

Customer: Hi! I think we're ready. I'll start with the house salad, please.

Waiter: Sure! And for your main course?

Customer: I'd like the grilled chicken sandwich with a side of fries.

Waiter: Great choice. And would you like something to drink?

Customer: Yes, I'll have an iced tea, please.

Waiter: Perfect. I'll get that started for you right away!

Scenario 2: Ordering at a Fancy Restaurant

Host: Good evening, do you have a reservation?

Customer: Yes, it's under "James."

Host: Ah, yes! Right this way, Mr. James. Here's your table.

Waiter: Good evening! May I start you off with something to drink?

Customer: I'll have a glass of the house red wine, please.

Waiter: Excellent choice. Are you ready to order your meal, or would you like to hear the specials?

Customer: I'd like to hear the specials, please.

Waiter: Certainly! Tonight, we have a seared salmon with a lemon butter sauce, served with asparagus and roasted potatoes.

Customer: That sounds delicious. I'll have the salmon.

Waiter: Very good. I'll be back shortly with your wine.

3. Asking About Dietary Restrictions and Food Allergies

Scenario 1: Allergies

Customer: Hi, before I order, I just want to check if there are any nuts in the pasta dishes.

Waiter: Let me check with the kitchen to be sure. Are you allergic to all nuts?

Customer: Yes, I have a severe allergy to peanuts and tree nuts.

Waiter: Understood. I'll confirm with the chef and let you know which dishes are safe.

(Waiter returns)

Waiter: Thank you for waiting. The chef confirmed that our pasta dishes do not contain nuts, but please avoid the pesto sauce, as it has pine nuts.

Customer: Great, thank you for checking. I'll have the spaghetti marinara.

Scenario 2: Dietary Restrictions

Customer: Hi, I'm vegan. Could you suggest some menu items that don't contain any animal products?

Waiter: Absolutely! We have a vegan salad with quinoa and roasted vegetables. The veggie burger is also vegan if you get it without the cheese and mayo.

Customer: I'll go with the veggie burger. Could I add avocado?

Waiter: Certainly! I'll note that down for the kitchen.

4. Dealing with Problems (Incorrect Orders, Complaints, Asking for the Bill)

Scenario 1: Incorrect Order

Customer: Excuse me, I ordered the Caesar salad, but this looks like a garden salad.

Waiter: Oh, I apologize for that! Let me take it back and have the kitchen prepare the Caesar salad for you.

Customer: Thank you.

(Waiter returns with correct order)

Waiter: Here's your Caesar salad. I'm so sorry for the mix-up.

Customer: No problem, thank you for fixing it so quickly.

Scenario 2: Complaints

Customer: Excuse me, but this steak is a bit overcooked. I asked for medium rare, and it seems well-done.

Waiter: I apologize, let me take it back to the kitchen and have them cook a new one for you. Would you like anything in the meantime?

Customer: No, that's okay. I'll wait, thank you.

(Waiter returns with a new steak)

Waiter: Here's your steak, cooked to medium rare. We've also taken it off the bill for the inconvenience.

Customer: I appreciate that, thank you.

Scenario 3: Asking for the Bill

Customer: Hi, we're ready for the check, please.

Waiter: Certainly. I'll bring it right over.

(Waiter returns with the bill)

Waiter: Here's your check. You can pay at the register when you're ready.

Customer: Thank you!

Scenario 4: Splitting the Bill

Customer 1: Could we split the bill?

Waiter: Absolutely. How would you like to divide it?

Customer 1: We'll just split it evenly.

Waiter: Got it. I'll bring two separate checks.

(Waiter returns with split bills)

Waiter: Here are your bills. You can each pay at the register whenever you're ready.

Customer 2: Perfect, thank you!

School and Education

Enrolling in Classes or Courses

Receptionist: Good morning! How can I help you today?

Student: Hi, I'd like to enroll in some classes for this semester.

Receptionist: Of course! Do you already know which courses you want to take?

Student: Yes, I'm interested in English Literature and Calculus.

Receptionist: Great! Can I have your student ID, please?

Student: Sure, here it is.

Receptionist: Thank you. Let me check if there are available spots in those courses.

Student: Okay, thank you.

Receptionist: It looks like there's room in both classes. Would you like to proceed with the enrollment?

Student: Yes, please.

Receptionist: All right, you're all set! You'll receive an email with the course schedule and other details.

Student: Perfect, thank you so much!

Receptionist: You're welcome! Have a great semester.

Vocabulary for School Settings (Subjects, Grades, Assignments)

Student 1: Hey, what class do you have next?

Student 2: I have History. It's actually pretty interesting this year.

Student 1: Lucky! I have Math, and I'm struggling with calculus.

Student 2: Maybe we could study together sometime. I'm pretty good at math.

Student 1: That'd be awesome! Oh, by the way, have you done the English assignment yet?

Student 2: Not yet. It's the essay on Shakespeare, right?

Student 1: Yeah, it's due on Friday. I haven't even started.

Student 2: Me neither! I guess we both need a study session.

Student 1: Definitely. Let's plan something for tomorrow.

Speaking with Teachers or Classmates

Teacher: Good morning, everyone. Today, we're going to start with a group discussion.

Student: What's the topic, Mr. Allen?

Teacher: We'll be discussing the impact of social media on young people.

Student: Should we work with the people sitting next to us?

Teacher: Yes, please. Each group will have 10 minutes to prepare.

Student: Okay, sounds good.

Classmate 1: Do you have any ideas on this topic?

Classmate 2: I think social media has both positive and negative effects. It helps people connect, but it can also be distracting.

Classmate 1: Good point. Let's start with the positive aspects and then discuss the drawbacks.

Parent-Teacher Meeting Scenarios

Teacher: Good afternoon, Mr. and Mrs. Smith. Thank you for coming in today.

Parent: Thank you for meeting with us. We wanted to discuss Emily's progress in school.

Teacher: Absolutely. Emily has been doing well in most subjects, especially English.

Parent: That's great to hear. Are there any areas she needs to work on?

Teacher: She could use a bit more practice in Math. We're covering some new concepts, and she seems a little hesitant.

Parent: Okay, we can help her at home. Do you have any suggestions?

Teacher: I recommend some extra practice with multiplication and division, just to build confidence.

Parent: Thanks for the advice. We'll make sure to focus on that.

School Events

Principal: Hello, everyone! Thank you all for coming to our annual school festival!

Parent: This looks amazing. My kids have been talking about this all week.

Principal: We're glad to hear that. We have activities for everyone, including games, a bake sale, and performances.

Student: Excuse me, where's the science fair happening?

Principal: The science fair is in the main gym. Just follow the signs.

Student: Thank you!

Parent: Do you have a schedule for the performances?

Principal: Yes, here you go. The choir will perform at 2 PM, followed by the drama club at 3 PM.

Parent: Thanks! This looks like it'll be a fun day.

Public Transportation and Directions

Asking for Directions and Basic Navigation

Conversation 1: Asking Directions on the Street

Alex: Excuse me, can you help me find the nearest subway station?

Local: Sure, it's about three blocks straight ahead. Look for the big blue "M" sign on your left.

Alex: Three blocks? Alright, got it. And is it the central line?

Local: Yes, that's right. It's the central line, and it will take you downtown.

Alex: Perfect, thank you so much!

Conversation 2: Directions Inside the Subway Station

Lina: Excuse me, is this the platform for the southbound train?

Staff: Yes, it is. You can take the southbound train from here.

Lina: Great! Do you know how many stops it is to Main Street?

Staff: Let me see... It's four stops from here. You'll be there in about 10 minutes.

Lina: Thank you! That's very helpful.

Vocabulary for Public Transport (Bus, Train, Subway)

Conversation 3: Understanding Bus Routes

Tourist: Hi, does this bus go to the airport?

Driver: No, you'll need to take Bus 65. This one only goes to the city center.

Tourist: I see. Where can I catch Bus 65?

Driver: There's a stop for it just across the street.

Tourist: Thanks! And does it run frequently?

Driver: Every 15 minutes during the day.

Conversation 4: Asking for Help on the Train

Marcus: Excuse me, do you know if this train goes to Riverdale?

Passenger: Yes, but only if you're on the express train. This one is a local.

Marcus: Oh, I didn't realize. How can I switch to the express?

Passenger: Get off at the next stop and wait for the express on Platform 2.

Marcus: Got it, thank you so much!

Buying Tickets and Understanding Schedules

Conversation 5: Buying a Ticket at the Bus Station

Ella: Hi, I'd like a ticket to Oakville, please.

Clerk: Sure thing. Do you want a one-way or round-trip ticket?

Ella: One-way, please. How much is it?

Clerk: That'll be $12.50. The next bus leaves in 15 minutes.

Ella: Perfect. Here's my payment.

Clerk: Thank you. Here's your ticket. The bus will be at Platform B.

Conversation 6: At the Train Station Ticket Counter

Ryan: Excuse me, I need a ticket to Green Valley.

Agent: Sure, Green Valley. Are you looking for the express train or the local?

Ryan: Which one is faster?

Agent: The express takes 40 minutes, and the local takes just over an hour.

Ryan: I'll go with the express, please.

Agent: Alright, that'll be $18.

Ryan: Thank you. Could you tell me what time it departs?

Agent: The next express train departs in 20 minutes from Platform 3.

Asking for Help When Lost or Confused

Conversation 7: Lost in a New City

Sam: Hi, I think I'm a little lost. Can you help me find Maple Street?

Pedestrian: Sure, you're actually not far. Go back two blocks, then make a right. Maple Street will be the third street on your left.

Sam: Thank you so much! I was starting to panic a little.

Pedestrian: No worries. Happens to everyone!

Conversation 8: Confused About a Subway Transfer

Claire: Excuse me, I'm trying to get to Riverside Station, but I'm not sure about the transfer.

Subway Employee: No problem. You'll take the Green Line from here, then switch to the Blue Line at Central Station.

Claire: So I transfer at Central, then take the Blue Line?

Subway Employee: Yes, exactly. Riverside will be three stops from there.

Claire: Thank you! I appreciate the help.

Conversation 9: Asking for Help on the Subway Platform

James: Excuse me, do you know if this train goes to Park Avenue?

Commuter: Yes, it does. It's the next stop after this one.

James: Oh, perfect! Thanks for confirming.

Commuter: No problem, happy to help.

Additional Vocabulary for Public Transport

Platform: Where passengers wait to board the train.

Ticket counter: Place where you purchase tickets.

One-way ticket: Ticket for a single trip.

Round-trip ticket: Ticket for going and returning.

Express train: A faster train with fewer stops.

Local train: A train that stops at all stations.

Transfer: Switching from one train/bus line to another.

Fare: The cost of a ticket.

Schedule: The timetable of transport services.

Technology and Social Media

1. Discussing Common Technology (Smartphones, Computers, Apps)

Emma: Hey, did you see the new smartphone that just launched?

Jake: I think I saw an ad. What's so special about it?

Emma: It's got a fantastic camera, even better than some professional ones. Plus, it has this crazy fast processor.

Jake: How's the battery life, though? My phone barely lasts a day with all the apps I use.

Emma: They claim it can go two full days with regular use.

Jake: That sounds great, but I bet it costs a fortune.

Emma: Yeah, it's definitely pricey. But you know how people are—they'll probably still line up to buy it.

2. Vocabulary for Social Media Platforms and Online Interactions

Sam: Are you on Threads yet? Everyone's moving there.

Mia: Yeah, I joined last week. It's like Twitter but way more laid-back.

Sam: I noticed that! You can post longer texts, too.

Mia: Exactly! I've been using it to share some of my travel stories. Do you post often?

Sam: I mostly stick to Instagram for photos. But on Threads, I just follow people and read updates.

Mia: Instagram's good for photos, but I like that Threads feels a bit more personal.

Sam: True, but I think each platform has its own vibe, don't you?

Mia: Absolutely. I'm careful to avoid over-sharing, though. You never know who's watching.

3. Talking about Privacy, Online Safety, and Handling Cyber Issues

Lily: I'm getting a bit paranoid about my privacy online lately.

Tom: What happened?

Lily: I got this email saying they have my personal data, and I had to pay to keep it private.

Tom: Sounds like a phishing scam. Did they ask for any of your details directly?

Lily: Yeah, they wanted my banking info, which was suspicious.

Tom: Definitely don't give out any information! Just report it as spam and ignore it.

Lily: I know, but it's scary. I think I'll also change my passwords just in case.

Tom: Good idea. And set up two-factor authentication on your accounts. It adds an extra layer of security.

Lily: I'll do that. It's crazy how careful we need to be online now.

4. Describing Technical Problems and Asking for Assistance

Anna: I can't seem to connect my laptop to the Wi-Fi. Any idea why?

Ben: Is the Wi-Fi on your other devices working?

Anna: Yeah, my phone and tablet are both connected.

Ben: Strange. Have you tried restarting your laptop?

Anna: I did, but it's still not connecting.

Ben: Check if the Wi-Fi driver is updated. Sometimes, it causes issues if it's outdated.

Anna: How do I do that? I'm not very tech-savvy.

Ben: Go to Device Manager, look for Network Adapters, then right-click on the Wi-Fi driver and choose "Update."

Anna: Okay, let me try that. Thanks for walking me through it!

5. Troubleshooting Common App Issues

Mark: My social media app keeps crashing every time I open it. What's going on?

Sara: Are you using the latest version? Sometimes, older versions crash.

Mark: I haven't updated it in a while. How do I check?

Sara: Go to the app store, and if there's an update available, you'll see it there.

Mark: Got it. I'll update it and see if it works.

Sara: If it still crashes, try clearing the app's cache in your settings.

Mark: Will that delete my data?

Sara: No, it'll just remove some temporary files. Your data should stay safe.

6. Discussing New Features on Social Media Platforms

Olivia: Did you notice the new stories feature on Instagram?

Lucas: Yeah, now you can reply with photos and videos directly to stories.

Olivia: I think it's pretty cool! Makes conversations more interactive.

Lucas: Definitely. But I find it a bit overwhelming. There are just so many features now.

Olivia: True, they're always adding something. I can barely keep up.

Lucas: Sometimes, I wish they'd just keep it simple.

7. Explaining Online Security Measures

Riley: I'm thinking about getting a VPN. Do you use one?

Mason: Yeah, it's good for protecting your data, especially on public Wi-Fi.

Riley: How does it work, exactly?

Mason: It encrypts your internet connection, so hackers can't see what you're doing.

Riley: Sounds like something everyone should use!

Mason: For sure. It's one of the easiest ways to keep your info private online.

8. Asking for Help with App Navigation

Ethan: I just joined TikTok, but I'm totally lost. Any tips?

Sophia: Sure! The main page shows videos based on your interests, and the "For You" page is where the most popular stuff appears.

Ethan: I noticed the "For You" page, but how do I find specific videos?

Sophia: Just use the search bar. Type in keywords, and it'll show related videos and creators.

Ethan: Got it. And how do I save videos?

Sophia: There should be a "Save" button below each video. Just tap it, and it'll be in your favorites.

9. Discussing the Impact of Social Media on Privacy

Clara: Have you ever thought about how much personal information we share online?

Leo: I try not to think about it, but yeah, it's a lot.

Clara: I read that companies sell our data to advertisers without us knowing.

Leo: That's why I'm cautious about what I post. You never know who's watching.

Clara: Me too. I don't even tag my location anymore.

Leo: Smart move. Better safe than sorry, right?

10. Helping with Email Issues

James: My email isn't sending messages, and it keeps saying, "Error connecting to server."

Nina: Could be an issue with the email server. Have you tried logging out and back in?

James: Not yet. I'll try that now.

Nina: Also, check if you're connected to Wi-Fi. Sometimes, a weak connection can cause errors.

James: Good point. I'll check my connection.

Nina: If it still doesn't work, try a different email app. It might just be an app glitch.

11. Discussing Privacy Settings on Social Media

Liam: Do you keep your social media profiles private?

Ella: Absolutely. Only my friends can see my posts.

Liam: I'm thinking of doing the same. People keep sending random friend requests.

Ella: Set your account to private, and you'll have more control.

Liam: I will. Thanks for the tip!

12. Troubleshooting Video Call Issues

Chris: I can't hear anything during my video calls. The audio just doesn't work.

Ava: Have you checked if the microphone is enabled on your computer?

Chris: Yeah, I did, but it's still not working.

Ava: Try switching to a different browser or app. Sometimes, the one you're using might have issues.

Chris: I'll give that a try. Thanks!

Leisure and Hobbies

Talking about Personal Interests and Hobbies

Conversation 1: Talking About Interests

Ava: Hey, Lucas, do you have any hobbies?

Lucas: Yeah, I'm really into photography. I love capturing landscapes and city scenes. What about you?

Ava: That sounds amazing! I'm more into arts and crafts. I like painting and making handmade jewelry.

Lucas: That's so cool! Do you sell your pieces or just keep them for yourself?

Ava: Mostly for myself, but I sometimes gift them to friends. Ever thought about doing a photography exhibition?

Lucas: Actually, that would be a dream. Maybe someday when I have a solid collection!

Conversation 2: Talking About Reading

Emma: I finally finished that novel you recommended!

Ben: Really? How'd you like it?

Emma: It was so intense! I couldn't put it down. The ending was a twist, though.

Ben: I know, right? That author has a way of surprising readers. Any new books on your list?

Emma: I'm thinking of starting a mystery series next. Have you read any good ones lately?

Ben: Not recently, but I heard the new one by Lee Thompson is great. Let's swap books when you're done!

Vocabulary for Activities

Conversation 3: Discussing Sports and Fitness Activities

Liam: Hey, do you play any sports, Sofia?

Sofia: Yeah, I play tennis on weekends. It's such a stress reliever! Do you play anything?

Liam: I've been trying to get into basketball lately. It's great exercise and a lot of fun.

Sofia: Nice! We should play a game together sometime. Tennis courts around here are always free on Sundays.

Liam: I'd love that. Do you play competitively, or is it more for fun?

Sofia: Mostly for fun. I'm not too serious about it, but I do enjoy staying active.

Making Plans with Friends for Activities and Events

Conversation 4: Planning a Movie Night

Oliver: Hey, Sarah, have you seen that new superhero movie everyone's talking about?

Sarah: No, I haven't, but I really want to! Are you planning to see it?

Oliver: Yes! Do you want to go this Friday?

Sarah: Sounds good to me. Should we invite anyone else?

Oliver: How about Ellie and Josh? They'd love it too.

Sarah: Perfect! Let's meet around 6, grab some snacks, and head to the theater.

Conversation 5: Planning a Hiking Trip

David: So, are we still on for the hiking trip this weekend?

Alex: Absolutely! I was just checking the trail map. It looks like a good challenge.

David: Awesome. Should we meet at the trailhead around 8 in the morning?

Alex: That works for me. Don't forget your water and snacks.

David: Already packed! Are we bringing lunch, or just keeping it light?

Alex: Let's keep it light. We can grab lunch after we're done.

Joining Clubs, Classes, or Groups Related to Hobbies

Conversation 6: Joining a Photography Class

Ella: Hey, are you still interested in learning more about photography?

Noah: Definitely! I've been practicing, but I feel like I could use some tips.

Ella: I just signed up for a beginner class. It's on Thursdays after work. Want to join me?

Noah: That sounds perfect! I'd love to join. Where's the class held?

Ella: At the community center downtown. It's pretty affordable, too.

Noah: I'm in! I'll sign up today. Thanks for letting me know.

Conversation 7: Joining a Book Club

Isabella: You know, I've been looking for a way to read more consistently.

James: Same here! I just joined a book club. It's been great for motivation.

Isabella: That's a great idea! How does it work?

James: We meet once a month, pick a book, and then discuss it together. It's relaxed but keeps you on track.

Isabella: That sounds fun! Can I join?

James: Of course! We're meeting this Friday if you're free.

Isabella: Count me in. Thanks for inviting me!

Shopping for Essentials

Shopping for Essentials

Scene 1: At the Grocery Store

Vocabulary Focus: Grocery Sections and Asking for Help

Customer: Excuse me, can you tell me where I can find the cereal?

Store Associate: Sure! It's in aisle 5, right next to the breakfast bars.

Customer: Thank you. Do you have gluten-free cereal options?

Store Associate: Yes, we do. They're on the top shelf in the same aisle. Look for the green labels.

Customer: Great, thanks! Also, I'm looking for fresh herbs. Do you have a section for that?

Store Associate: Yes, you'll find fresh herbs in the produce section, near the vegetables. Let me know if you need more help.

Scene 2: Pharmacy

Vocabulary Focus: Medication and Health Products

Customer: Hi, I need some pain relievers. Could you show me where they are?

Pharmacist: Of course. We have pain relievers in aisle 3. Are you looking for tablets or something topical?

Customer: Tablets, please. And do you have anything for allergies?

Pharmacist: Yes, we carry a range of allergy medications. They're in the same aisle, right beside the cold and flu products.

Customer: Thanks. Do you have non-drowsy options?

Pharmacist: Absolutely. You'll see some labeled as non-drowsy. Just let me know if you need help choosing one.

Scene 3: Comparing Prices and Quality

Vocabulary Focus: Fruits and Vegetables

Customer 1: Look at these apples. They're on sale for $1.99 per pound.

Customer 2: That's a good price. Do you think they're organic?

Customer 1: No, it doesn't look like it. The organic ones are usually labeled. Let's ask.

Store Associate: Hi, can I help you with anything?

Customer 1: Yes, are these apples organic?

Store Associate: No, they're conventional. Our organic produce is in the next aisle.

Customer 2: Thanks. Do you know the price for the organic apples?

Store Associate: They're $2.99 per pound.

Customer 1: A bit more expensive, but it's worth it for organic.

Customer 2: Agreed. Let's grab a few.

Scene 4: Handling Returns

Vocabulary Focus: Refund and Exchange

Customer: Hi, I'd like to return these shoes. They don't fit well.

Store Clerk: Certainly. Do you have the receipt?

Customer: Yes, here it is.

Store Clerk: Thank you. Would you like a refund or an exchange?

Customer: A refund, please.

Store Clerk: No problem. I'll process that for you. You should see the amount back on your card within 3–5 business days.

Customer: Thank you!

Scene 5: Talking about Deals and Discounts

Vocabulary Focus: Discounts and Payment Methods

Customer: Excuse me, I saw a sign for 10% off on skincare products. Does that include all brands?

Store Associate: Yes, the discount applies to all skincare items.

Customer: Perfect. And do you accept digital wallets, like Apple Pay?

Store Associate: Yes, we accept Apple Pay, Google Pay, and other digital wallets.

Customer: Great, thank you. I'll get this moisturizer, then.

Store Associate: Sure thing. With the 10% off, your total comes to $18.00.

Customer: Perfect. I'll pay with Apple Pay.

Revision

Daily Routines

Morning Routine

A: Good morning! Did you sleep well?

B: Not really, I kept tossing and turning.

A: I know the feeling. What's for breakfast?

B: I'm thinking of having some eggs and toast. How about you?

A: I'll just grab a smoothie and head out.

Weather Talk

A: It looks like it might rain today.

B: Really? I didn't check the forecast.

A: Yeah, you might want to take an umbrella.

B: Good idea! I hate getting caught in the rain.

Shopping

Supermarket Conversations

A: Excuse me, where can I find the pasta?

B: Aisle 5, right next to the rice.

A: Thanks! Do you know if they have gluten-free options?

B: Yes, they do! Just look for the marked shelf.

At the Cash Register

A: Hi there! How much is this?

B: That's $5.99.

A: Can I pay with a credit card?

B: Sure! Just swipe it here.

Traveling

Booking Tickets

A: I'd like to book a ticket to New York, please.

B: One way or round trip?

A: Round trip, please.

B: That'll be $300. Would you like to add insurance?

Asking for Directions

A: Excuse me, can you help me?

B: Sure! Where do you need to go?

A: I'm looking for Central Park.

B: Just go straight and take the second left.

At Work

Office Introductions

A: Hi, I'm Alex. I just started here.

B: Nice to meet you, Alex! I'm Jamie.

A: What department are you in?

B: I work in marketing. How about you?

Meeting Conversations

A: Can everyone please share their updates?

B: I've completed the project ahead of schedule.

C: I'm still working on mine; I hit a few roadblocks.

A: Let's discuss those challenges later.

Socializing

Meeting New People

A: Hi! I'm Sarah. What's your name?

B: I'm Tom. Nice to meet you!

A: What do you do for fun?

B: I love hiking and photography. How about you?

Inviting Friends

A: Do you want to grab coffee this weekend?

B: That sounds great! What time?

A: How about Saturday at 10?

B: Perfect! See you then.

Health and Emergencies

At the Doctor's Office

A: Hello, I have an appointment at 3 PM.

B: Name, please?

A: It's Jordan Smith.

B: Great! Please take a seat, the doctor will see you shortly.

Handling Emergencies

A: Help! I think I've lost my wallet.

B: Have you checked your pockets?

A: Yes, I did! I can't find it anywhere.

B: Let's report it to lost and found right away.

Dealing with Problems

Customer Service Complaint

A: Hi, I received the wrong order.

B: I'm sorry to hear that. What did you order?

A: I ordered a vegetarian pizza, but I got a pepperoni one.

B: Let me fix that for you right away!

Service Issue

A: Excuse me, my internet isn't working.

B: Let me check that for you.

A: Thank you! I need it for a meeting later.

B: It looks like there's an outage in your area.

Phrases and Expressions

Common Idioms

A: I heard you got a promotion! Congratulations!

B: Thanks! I'm over the moon!

A: That's awesome! You really deserve it.

B: I appreciate that!

Politeness and Respect
A: Would you mind helping me with this?
B: Not at all! What do you need?
A: I'm having trouble with this report.
B: I'd be happy to take a look.